The Crash of 1929

Look for these and other exciting
World Disasters books:

Pompeii
The Black Death
The Titanic
The Dust Bowl
The Chicago Fire
The Armenian Earthquake
The San Francisco Earthquake

The
Crash
of 1929

by Ronald Migneco and Timothy Levi Biel

Illustrations by Maurie Manning
and
Michael Spackman
Robert Caldwell
Randol Eagles

LUCENT
B·O·O·K·S

WORLD DISASTERS

Library of Congress Cataloging-in-Publication Data
Migneco, Ronald, 1954-, and Biel, Timothy, 1950-
    Crash of 1929/by Ronald Migneco and Timothy Biel; illustrations by Maurie Manning.
      p.   cm. -- (World disasters)
    Bibliography: p.
    Includes index.
    Summary: An account of the stock market crash of 1929.
    ISBN 1-56006-003-4
    1. Depressions--1929--United States--1918-1945--Juvenile literature. [1. Depressions--1929. 2. U.S.--Economic conditions.] I. Manning, Maurie, 1960- ill. II. Title: Crash of 1929. III. Series.
HB3717 1929.M53 1989
338.5'4'097309043--dc20
                                            89-33556
                                              CIP
                                              AC

To Melanie

Table of Contents

Preface

The World Disasters Series

World disasters have always aroused human curiosity. Whenever news of tragedy spreads, we want to learn more about it. We wonder how and why the disaster happened, how people reacted, and whether we might have acted differently. To be sure, disaster evokes a wide range of responses—fear, sorrow, despair, generosity, even hope. Yet from every great disaster, one remarkable truth always seems to emerge: in spite of death, pain, and destruction, the human spirit triumphs.

History is full of great disasters, which arise from a variety of causes. Earthquakes, floods, volcanic eruptions, and other natural events often produce widespread destruction. Just as often, however, people accidentally bring suffering and distress on themselves and other human beings. And many disasters have sinister causes, like human greed, envy, or prejudice.

The disasters included in this series have been chosen not only for their dramatic qualities, but also for their educational value. The reader will learn about the causes and effects of the greatest disasters in history. Technical concepts and interesting anecdotes are explained and illustrated in inset boxes.

But disasters should not be viewed in isolation. To enrich the reader's understanding, these books present historical information about the time period, and interesting facts about the culture in which each disaster occurred. Finally, they teach valuable lessons about human nature. More acts of bravery, cowardice, intelligence, and foolishness are compressed into the few days of a disaster than most people experience in a lifetime.

Dramatic illustrations and evocative narrative lure the reader to distant cities and times gone by. Readers witness the awesome power of an exploding volcano, the magnitude of a violent earthquake, and the hopelessness of passengers on a mighty ship passing to its watery grave. By reliving the events, the reader will see how disaster affects the lives of real people and will gain a deeper understanding of their sorrow, their pain, their courage, and their hope.

Introduction
End of an Era

The Roaring Twenties, from 1920 through 1929, was an exciting period in American history. Following World War I, the people of the United States experienced the pride and confidence that arise from living in the world's wealthiest and most powerful nation.

Much of this confidence came from the strength of American business. Industry was booming. Railroads and automobiles crisscrossed the nation. Even the fledgling airline industry was taking off.

One reason for this progress was the revolutionary new role of the stock market. Large corporations needed enough money to build automated factories and to distribute their products around the world. Most of this money came from investors who bought stock in the corporations. As the corporations grew, the stock market boomed, turning many investors into new millionaires almost overnight.

As a result, investment fever swept the nation. Alongside the entrepreneurs and industrialists, working men and women began to try their luck on Wall Street. They withdrew their savings from banks to buy stocks. Many of them even borrowed heavily to invest in the stock market. They believed that America had entered an age of permanent prosperity. Sooner or later, the opportunity to become wealthy would be open to every American.

In 1929, the prices of stocks were still rising, and people were still investing. On street corners and park benches,

in buses and subways, people spoke knowingly of "the price of RCA stock," and "the Dow Jones industrial average." So much money was pouring into the stock market that stock prices rose unrealistically. Some financial experts began to warn that stock prices were too high. Despite the warnings, heavy investment in the stock market continued. People seemed to believe that stock prices could rise forever.

But in the fall of 1929, a series of events finally convinced many investors that stock prices were not going much higher. On Thursday, October 24, a number of major investors began to sell their stock. But they could not find enough buyers interested in paying the unrealistically high stock prices. So the prices began to fall. Unfortunately, when investors saw this, many of them panicked. The more investors tried to sell, the harder it became to find buyers, and the faster the prices fell. This notorious day in America's economic history has become known as Black Thursday. By Tuesday, October 29, just five days later, stock prices had fallen even farther, ending any hope of a quick recovery.

Many Americans lost their confidence in the stock market. Without investors, corporate production and earnings fell. Many people lost their jobs. The Great Depression, a terrible cycle of unemployment and declining production gripped the nation. The era of permanent prosperity had not even lasted a decade. Its fate had been sealed by the Crash of 1929.

The Crash of 1929's Place in History

——— American Revolution—1776

——— New York Stock Exchange is organized—1791

——— War of 1812—1812-1814

——— Gold is discovered in California—1848

——— Financial panic strikes New York—1857
——— American Civil War—1861-1865
——— Wall Street's first "Black Friday"—1869
——— Alexander Graham Bell patents telephone—1876

——— World's first gasoline-powered vehicle—1885

——— First Ford motorcar—1893

——— New York Stock Exchange completed—1903

——— World War I—1914-1917
RCA is founded—1919
Prohibition becomes law—1920
Stock Market Crash—1929
SEC is created—1934
——— World War II—1939-1945

——— American Stock Exchange is created—1953

——— John F. Kennedy assassinated—1963
——— Neil Armstrong walks on the moon—1969

——— Ninety Americans taken hostage in Iran—1979

——— Stock Market Crash—1987

One
The Roaring Twenties

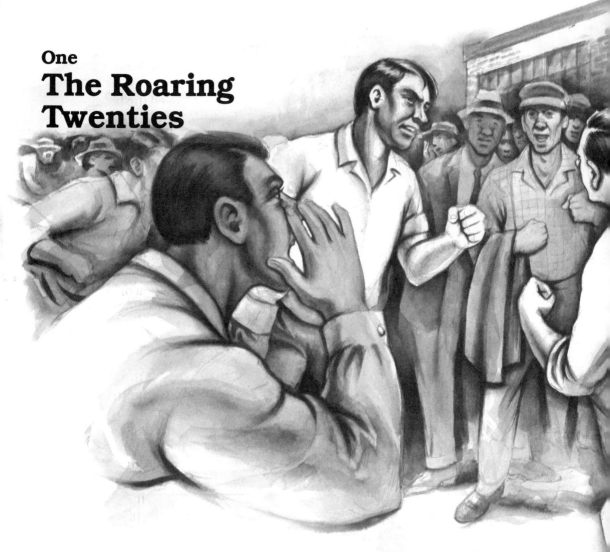

On the day after New Year's in 1929, Henry Ford, builder of the first American automobile and inventor of the assembly line, stood at a second-story window in his brand new auto plant in Detroit, Michigan. He watched as thousands of men crowded toward the front of the plant. Near the door, a fight broke out among three or four men, each trying to be the first one inside. In the next few days, Ford would be hiring an additional thirty thousand employees to meet the unbelievable demand for Ford's newest car, the Model A.

Turning his back on the activity, Ford peered through an interior window onto the vast assembly room below him. There, men dressed in white and blue overalls attached parts to the jet black car frames that glided past on the world's most automated assembly line.

Henry Ford had every reason to feel content with his accomplishments, but at this moment he wore a scowl on his face. Far too many people—over one

ing since 1922, but now it seemed to be slowing down.

Henry Ford blamed the bankers and **brokers** of **Wall Street**, the men who controlled the **stock market** for this slowdown. As usual, he found a way to make his opinion known. When newspaper reporters came to see his new plant in operation, he took advantage of the opportunity to blast the Wall Street establishment.

No businessman in America managed to capture the public attention the way Ford did. Whatever words he spoke in public were eagerly lapped up by the press. Ford reminded the reporters that everything they saw at the plant, as well as the entire Ford empire, had been built "without a penny from the **pariahs** of Wall Street." He also announced that in the coming October he would celebrate "one of the most spectacular events of the decade." That is when he planned the grand opening of his American Village, a theme park celebrating great moments in American history.

At age sixty-five, Henry Ford was a living legend. His ingenuity had endeared him to the American public. His invention of the assembly line was transforming American industry. Now the public cheered his idea for the American Village.

However, when he warned the public about the dangers of speculating on the stock market, many Americans ignored him. To them, buying **stocks** in American **corporations** was a sensible thing to do. The 1920s had been a prosperous decade. Although an enormous gap still existed between the rich and the poor, almost everyone's standard of living had steadily improved.

hundred thousand—had applied for the new jobs at the plant. Many may have been attracted by the excellent wage of 62$\frac{1}{2}$ cents per hour. But Ford suspected another reason for the huge turnout. He believed it was a sign that unemployment was rising in the nation. The American economy had been booming since 1922, but now it seemed to be

The manufacturing industry was booming. The number of factories in the United States grew from about 180,000 in 1925 to more than 200,000 by 1929. And during the same period, the value of their products increased from about $60 billion to nearly $70 billion.

As the economy grew, business costs skyrocketed. The production of automobiles, trucks, railroads, steamships, and airplanes demanded large factories and enormous amounts of **capital**, or money used to operate a business. At the same time, the transportation industry and the emerging radio industry were bringing the different regions of the country closer together. Information and products were distributed farther and faster than ever before. The nation was becoming one vast market. Producing, advertising, and selling to this market was expensive.

WHAT ARE STOCKS?

Stocks are shares of ownership in a *corporation*. A corporation sells stock as a way to raise *capital*, or operating money. The people who buy stock in the corporation become its *stockholders* or *shareholders*. They are the owners of the corporation. They vote on major company issues and share the profits.

The company's stock is divided into equal *shares*. Every share that a stockholder owns entitles him or her to one vote. Thus a stockholder who owns ten shares has ten votes, while a stockholder with only one share has only one vote. Similarly, when the profits are divided among shareholders, the owner of ten shares would receive exactly ten times as much money as the owner of one share.

Becoming a **public corporation** was the only way most national and international companies could accumulate enough capital to produce and compete. Public corporations accumulate capital by selling stock, or shares of ownership, through public **stock**

HOW ARE STOCKS SOLD?

Stock in a public corporation must be bought or sold through a licensed stockbroker. There is no set price for stocks. Rather, the price is reached by agreement between two brokers at a stock exchange, one representing the buyer and the other representing the seller.

Suppose, for example, that Mr. Lopez in Los Angeles decides to buy one hundred shares of Supertronics, Inc., which is sold on the New York Stock Exchange. He calls his broker and tells her to buy 100 Supertronics, Inc. at the best available price. Mr. Lopez' order is then telephoned to the floor of the exchange in New York, where a telephone clerk relays the order to the floor broker.

Meanwhile, a Mrs. Commons in Boston has decided to sell one hundred shares of Supertronics. She orders her broker in Boston to sell one hundred shares at the best possible price. Mrs. Commons' sell order is then phoned to New York to a clerk at the stock exchange who relays it to another floor broker.

Both Mr. Lopez' broker and Mrs. Commons' broker head for the trading post where stock in Supertronics, Inc. is sold. There they ask, "How's Supertronics?' A specialist stationed at the post answers, "50-1/4 bid, 50-5/8 offer." This means

exchanges. These exchanges are generally called the stock market. By selling stock, corporations could take in large quantities of money to help them operate. The people who bought the stock, the **stockholders**, earned a share of the corporations' profit.

the highest anyone seems willing to pay for the stock is 50-1/4 ($50.25) per share, and the lowest anyone is offering to sell it for is 50-5/8 ($50.63) per share.

Mr. Lopez' broker announces that he will bid 50-3/8 ($50.38) per share for 100 shares of Supertronics. Hearing this, Mrs. Commons' broker offers to sell 100 shares for 50-3/8 per share. The two brokers agree on this compromise and report the sale to a clerk at the trading post.

The clerk, in turn, reports the sale to the telephone clerks, who report to the brokers in Los Angeles and Boston, who report to Mr. Lopez and Mrs. Commons, respectively, that their orders have been satisfied at 50-3/8.

In theory at least, stockholders usually have voting privileges on major policy decisions. Each stockholder is entitled to one vote for each share of stock he or she owns. In reality, important decisions are usually made by the company's board of directors, a small group of stockholders who control the majority of voting shares.

In the 1920s, the stock market was becoming an increasingly important part of the economy. There has never been another time like the 1920s in American industry and business. The economy was growing and changing so rapidly that even men responsible for the changes could not keep up with them.

By introducing mass production to the economy, Ford helped create a need for mass marketing, mass distributing, and mass capitalizing. Public corporations helped to supply the needed capital. Whether people like Henry Ford approved or not, the increasing power of the stock market was inevitable.

Investments in the stock market helped stimulate the economy, but late in the 1920s, a change was taking place in investment strategy. Instead of buying stock as a way to share in a company's profits, people were buying more and more stock on **speculation**. Rather than waiting to make money through **dividends**, or shares of the profit, speculators aimed to profit on the increasing value of the stock itself.

It was this strategy that worried people like Henry Ford. He feared that speculators had no interest in a company's long-term health and profitability. They only cared that a company's short-term profits were high, because that would make the price of its stock go up.

With the economy expanding, as it had throughout the twenties, speculating on the stock market had been extremely profitable. It was not only wealthy bankers and brokers who profited, but small investors, too. The enthusiasm for buying stock had spread to factory workers, housemaids, and elevator attendants. Stories circulated everywhere about the waitress who, overhearing a tip from one broker to another, made thirty thousand dollars overnight, the cab driver who became a millionaire, and the elderly widow who, trusting her broker's hunch, had made enough money to live comfortably for the rest of her life.

Such success stories were abundant in the twenties, and people were full of optimism. In December 1928, outgoing

President Calvin Coolidge expressed this optimism in his final State of the Union Address:

> *No Congress of the United States ever assembled, on surveying the state of the Union, has met with a more pleasing prospect than that which appears at the present time. In the domestic field there is tranquility and contentment...and the highest record of years of prosperity.... We may regard the present with satisfaction and anticipate the future with optimism.... The main source of these unexampled blessings lies in the integrity and character of the American people.*

Coolidge's outlook was echoed throughout the country. It was evident not only in the factories and the marketplaces, but in every facet of American life. This was the period that became known as the Roaring Twenties. Cars became faster and fancier. They came equipped with radios, interior heaters, and upholstered seats. The trendsetters bought roadsters decked with gleaming chrome.

Many young adults adopted a brash and daring outlook. Young women who openly defied proper manners and dress became known as *flappers*. They cut their hair short, wore bright red rouge and lipstick, donned short, slinky dresses, and draped long strings of beads over their bare necks. These young women and their escorts danced the Charleston to the lively sounds of jazz.

Prohibition, a national law that made the sale and consumption of liquor illegal, had been in effect since 1920, yet a great many Americans bought or manufactured their own "bootleg liquor." Liquor was also sold in illegal taverns, called *speakeasies*, that were frequented by even the most upstanding citizens in towns and cities across the country.

The motion picture industry also had a strong influence on the styles and manners of the twenties. In movie theaters everywhere, Americans watched stars such as Charlie Chaplin, Rudolph Valentino, and Mary Pickford. In 1929, Al Jolson starred in the first "talkie," *The Jazz Singer*.

Movies helped break down regional barriers and promote a national image, but it was radio, more than anything else, that created a national market. Regular broadcasts did not begin much before 1920, but by 1929 almost every American home had a radio. Sitting in their living rooms, Americans listened to advertisers urging them to buy the latest models of cars, refrigerators, and vacuum cleaners. They were told to buy the newest styles in clothes and to smoke cigarettes because it was fashionable.

William Durant

factory workers employed. Spending was practically a patriotic duty.

Amid the buying binge of the twenties, speculators in the stock market watched their profits grow. The dream of every speculator was to have the kind of success enjoyed by William C. Durant, one of the wealthiest and best-known speculators on Wall Street.

Like Henry Ford, Durant began his career in the automobile industry in Detroit. In fact, as the founder of General Motors (GM), he had been Ford's most serious rival. From these very similar starting places, however, Durant and Ford followed two extremely different routes to fame and fortune. Unlike Ford Motor Company, GM became a public corporation. During the time that Durant was with the company, he had numerous disagreements with other members of the board of directors. Finally, in 1920, GM had a dismal year in car sales. As its profits fell, so did the value of its stock. Durant, who owned a controlling interest of GM stock, lost over $120 million. He also lost his controlling interest in the company, and his enemies on the board of directors forced him to resign.

Although Durant had many enemies in the automobile industry, he had many friends who were powerful bankers and stockbrokers on Wall Street. In 1920, some of Durant's friends arranged the financing for him to begin speculating in the stock market. With his keen business sense, Durant was quick to recognize corporations with promise. He would buy stocks in these corporations when they were new or undiscovered, and the price was relatively low. Then, as the companies' earnings increased, so did the value of its stocks. Some esti-

Perhaps the greatest expression of optimism in the 1920s was the expanding role of credit. Borrowing money to buy a home, or even a car, had been common practice for years, but the idea of "buying now and paying later" for appliances, vacations, and other frills was entirely new. Americans were saving less and spending more, and very few people advised against it. People knew that buying products kept factories producing, and busy factories kept

mated that in just three months of speculating, Durant made fifty million dollars.

Soon the very fact that Durant purchased stock in a company was enough to drive up the value of that stock. Durant realized that by pooling the resources of several wealthy investors, he could influence which stocks rose and which ones fell. So he joined forces with some of the most powerful investors in America. Men like J.P. Morgan Jr., Percy Rockefeller, and Charles Mitchell, president of National City Bank, teamed with Durant to invest billions of dollars into selected stocks. As soon as they did, millions of other investors followed, and the prices of these stocks soared. The January 19, 1929, issue of *Collier's* magazine reported:

> *In Wall Street it is believed that William Durant has made more money out of this market than any other operator. The estimates run all the way from $100 million up.*

Both William Durant and Henry Ford became legends in their own time. Perhaps no two men better represented the unique place of the 1920s in economic history. It was a period in which two economic eras met head on.

The twenties marked the passing of the era of the independent **entrepreneur** like Henry Ford, who was part inventor and part business tycoon. Ford knew the business he owned forward and backward. He was as comfortable on the assembly line as he was in the board room. William Durant represented the new era of corporate ownership. He was not a manager, but an investor. For him, ownership had little to do with managing

a company or knowing the secrets of its success. Ownership was a matter of numbers, profits, and projected earnings. Success was a question of timing, knowing when to buy stock and when to sell it. As the 1920s came to a close, the clash between these two eras would affect the lives not only of Henry Ford and William Durant, but of almost every American since the Roaring Twenties.

Two
A Raging Bull

Wall Street, on Manhattan Island in New York City, is only seven blocks long. Yet to this day, as in 1929, it is the financial hub of the world. On the west, Wall Street ends at the old Trinity Church, and on the east it ends at the East River. One block from Trinity Church stands the New York Stock Exchange. Between the stock exchange and the East River are several of the world's largest banks, finance companies, and brokerages. In 1929, six of the ten largest banks in the world were located there. Right next door to the stock exchange, at 23 Wall Street, stood the House of Morgan, home of J.P. Morgan and Company, perhaps the most prestigious finance company in the world.

The stock exchange building is situated on the corner of Wall and Broad streets. The front of the building, with its marble steps and Greek columns, faces Broad Street. Along Wall Street is the entrance to the twenty-two-story tower that was added to the stock exchange in 1923.

On Tuesday morning, March 12, 1929, a crowd gathered around the stock exchange. This had been happening often in recent weeks. Whenever rumors

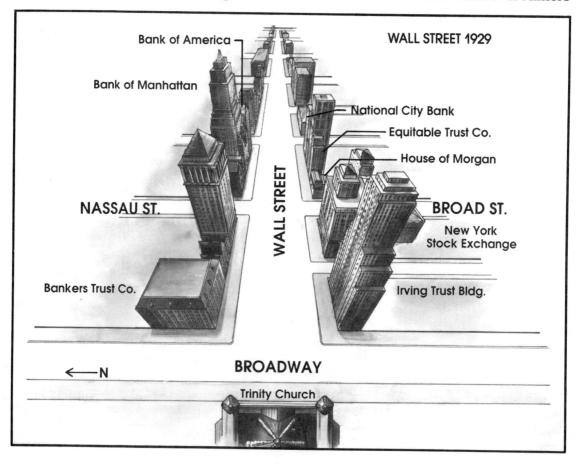

Bank of America
Bank of Manhattan
WALL STREET 1929
National City Bank
Equitable Trust Co.
House of Morgan
NASSAU ST.
WALL STREET
BROAD ST.
New York Stock Exchange
Bankers Trust Co.
Irving Trust Bldg.
←—N
BROADWAY
Trinity Church

spread that something out of the ordinary was happening on the stock market, people would crowd into the visitors gallery at the stock exchange. Thousands of others would go directly to their brokers' offices so they could see the results of **trade** activity as it was reported on **ticker tape** machines, or **tickers**. If a sudden opportunity arose to make money, investors wanted to act quickly.

On this Tuesday, rumors had spread that a group of investors was about to buy a large share of RCA, Radio Corporation of America. Prices in RCA stock were expected to climb over $100 a share. What the public did not know was that a week earlier, a select group of investors, including William Durant, Percy Rockefeller, John J. Raskob (who financed the construction of the Empire State Building), and Walter Chrysler, had all received a three-page document marked "Private and Confidential." Inside, the document bore the following heading:

Radio Corporation of America
Common Stock Syndicate
New Stock

The document described a carefully conceived plan to create a **trading pool**, a secretive plan to manipulate large quantities of stock in order to influence stock prices. Trading pools gave their participants—usually big investors—an unfair advantage in the stock market. Technically, trading pools were against the rules of most public stock exchanges, but with caution they could still be formed legally in 1929.

At that time there was very little government regulation of the stock market. The rules and regulations of each stock exchange were set and monitored by its members. For example, each of the 1,375 brokers who owned **seats** on the New York Stock Exchange agreed to conduct business according to its rules and regulations. A seat on the stock exchange is not actually a place to sit. It is a membership entitling a broker to trade on the exchange floor. In 1929, a seat on the New York Stock Exchange sold for about $600,000.

THE PRICE OF STOCK

Stock prices go up and down rather unpredictably. For the most part, however, they reflect the law of supply and demand. When many people want to buy stock in a certain company, they are willing to pay more to get it. The demand drives the price up. On the other hand, if more people want to sell the stock than buy it, the abundance of stocks for sale brings the price down.

Demand for the stock may rise because a company reports good earnings, announces an innovative new product which is expected to sell well, or merges with another successful company. It may also go up just because other stocks are going up and there is a general optimism about the economy. Demand for stock may drop because a company reports a decline or loss in earnings or announces a reorganization that will reduce profits. Or it may go down just because other stocks are going down and there is a lack of confidence about the state of the economy.

Because prices can change suddenly, knowing the most current price of a certain stock and whether the price is rising or falling is extremely important to investors. That is why most stock exchanges make up-to-the-minute stock *quotations* available to brokers everywhere in the country. Today these quotations are sent electronically, by computer. In 1929, they were sent by telegraph and recorded on *ticker tape* machines at brokerage houses throughout the United States and other countries.

New York Stock Exchange Archives

Trading room of the New York Stock Exchange as it looked in 1929.

The RCA pool had been carefully planned by one of Wall Street's shrewdest brokers. His name was Michael J. Meehan, and he had earned the name "king of radio" for his mastery of stocks in RCA and other corporations in this promising new field. Meehan's plan was to flood the market with high bids for RCA stock. Once other investors saw the price of RCA climbing, they would start buying, driving its price still higher. At a predetermined time, members of the pool would sell their stock for a handsome profit. Of course, this surge of sales would end the demand for the stock. As a result, its value would begin to drop, leaving other investors to take the loss.

Just one year earlier, Meehan had engineered another highly successful RCA trading pool, so this time he had no trouble getting other investors to participate. Raskob contributed $1 million to the pool. Durant and Walter Chrysler each added $500,000, as did brokers Bradford Ellsworth, Thomas Bragg, and Ben Smith. Altogether, Meehan received contributions from sixty-eight investors totalling nearly $13 million. The pool looked like such a sure thing that John Raskob even convinced his friend James Riordan to join in. Riordan was a millionaire, but he was neither as wealthy nor as adventurous as Raskob and the others.

In the following days, rumors had

mysteriously appeared in financial columns of newspapers around the country that an organized bid for large shares of RCA stock was about to take place. The news leaks were exactly what Meehan hoped for. By Tuesday, millions of stock market observers were waiting for RCA stocks to make their first upward movement. Many of them had come to the New York Stock Exchange to see it for themselves.

The best place to view the activity in the trading room of the New York Stock Exchange was from the third floor visitors' gallery. The gallery overlooked the immense trading room, which was nearly two-thirds as large as a football field. Five stories above the trading room floor, a great glass dome covered the room. Before the start of trading, brokers circulated through the trading room, anticipating their first trades and making mental notes about the current prices of their most frequently traded stocks.

Each broker wore an identification badge with a number on it. This number corresponded to one of the numbers on the giant **annunciator board** set into the marble wall above the entrance to the trading floor. The huge board was covered with hundreds of small shutters, and underneath each shutter was a number. Whenever a clerk had a message for a particular broker, he could push a button that electrically opened the shutter revealing that broker's number.

Scattered throughout the trading room were eighteen oval booths known as **trading posts**. At each post, stocks for specific companies were traded. The clerks and uniformed **pages** were stationed at these posts and at other booths located around the outer rim of the trading troom. The clerks at the outer booths usually worked for **brokerage houses**. Their main job was to take telephone orders from their brokerage house and relay them to those brokers on the floor who worked for the same house.

On Tuesday, March 12, before the market opened, Michael Meehan met with brokers Ben Smith, Brad Ellsworth, and Thomas Bragg in Bragg's Wall Street office. Meehan was a short, potbellied man with steel-rimmed glasses. His casual manner and style of dress disguised his ruthless business style. Just fifteen years before, Meehan had been a theater usher earning only about five thousand dollars a year. Now he was possibly the best-known broker in America.

BULL MARKETS AND BEAR MARKETS

When people talk about the stock market and call it a *bull market*, that means stock prices are steadily rising. If it is called a *bear market*, that means stock prices are steadily dropping. The names come from the way the two animals attack. A bull throws its victims up in the air, so a bull market means prices are rising. A bear knocks its victims down, so a bear market means falling prices.

People who invest in the stock market are also sometimes called bulls and bears. They are called bulls when they expect stock prices to go up and bears when they expect prices to go down.

As the master mind behind the planned pool, Meehan would not be directly involved with any of the buying or selling of RCA. The overall strategy would be handled by Tom Bragg. Bragg looked and talked like a prize fighter. His enemies said he smiled only when he collected a check from them. A veteran manipulator of the market, he would remain in his office and issue orders to Ellsworth by phone. Brad Ellsworth and Ben Smith would be on the trading room floor. Coordinating their buy and sell orders through Bragg, they would take care not to be seen together on the exchange floor.

At about 9:00 A.M., Michael Meehan appeared at the stock exchange. He walked to Trading Post Twelve, where RCA stock was traded. There he spoke to a broker who worked for his firm. The broker would be handling most of the buy or sell orders for RCA stock that Smith or Ellsworth requested.

At precisely 10:00 A.M., the gong sounded, signalling the opening of trade. Quickly the hum of conversation rose to a steady roar. To Meehan, the shrill-pitched yells and cheers had a satisfying ring to them. It meant the first prices of the day were up. It appeared to be another good day for the market.

The gong's echo had barely faded when Smith and Ellsworth placed their first orders for RCA stock with a broker from Meehan's company. Meehan watched as a clerk at Post Twelve changed the signs at the top of the post to show the new prices of the stocks traded at that post. Meehan could see at once that RCA was moving up.

Clerks at the trading posts wrote the information about every sale on a slip of paper. These slips were placed in **pneumatic tubes** and sent to ticker tape operators. From there, the same information, including the latest selling and asking prices of the traded stock, was entered into a telegraph system and printed on thousands of tickers throughout the country.

At about 10:30 A.M., one of the pool's brokers placed the first big buy order, for five thousand shares. Within thirty seconds, news of the blockbuster order was flashing across the ticker. Soon afterward, Bragg contacted Smith on the floor by phone. He ordered another thousand shares, this time in the name of his wife. As news spread that RCA had climbed to a new high of 92$^7/_8$ **points**, or dollars, orders to buy poured in from as far away as San Francisco, Miami, Seattle, and Chicago.

At regular intervals throughout the morning, William Durant checked the ticker in his Manhattan office. It looked as though his investment in the pool was showing a slight profit. By the end of the day, RCA stock stood at 91$^5/_8$, only a modest gain. But more importantly, a picture of great demand for the stock was being spread nationwide.

The next day, March 13, *The Wall Street Journal* reported:

> *RCA stock has gone to fresh record levels on the activities of big operators who have sponsored Radio's market for the last several weeks.*

For the rest of the week, Meehan's pool operators skillfully manipulated the demand for RCA stock. By Saturday, March 16, it had reached its peak of 109$^1/_4$. Only the members of the pool knew that this was the peak, for on Sunday they decided it was time to "pull the plug."

On Monday, Smith and Ellsworth began selling RCA stock. By the end of the day it had dropped back to 101. At that price it was eagerly snapped up by the unsuspecting public. Three days later, the stock had dropped further to 92$^1/_2$ as the pool managers completed unloading their shares.

As small investors across the country tried to recover their losses by selling, RCA dropped further to 87¼. Many of these investors lost thousands of dollars. Some went broke. But for the participants in Meehan's syndicate, the pool had been an enormous success.

For his $1 million investment, John Raskob made $300,000. His reluctant friend, James Riordan, earned about $60,000. Chrysler, Durant, and other investors made about $150,000 each. The biggest winner of all was Meehan. He made $650,000 in the stock sales, and his brokerage firm another $600,000 in commissions.

Lured by the prospect of making a fortune as Michael Meehan, William Durant, and others had, millions of Americans put their savings into stocks. By spring 1929, about two million American families had invested in the stock market. As long as stock prices continued to rise, their profits grew. A market in which stock prices are rising is called a **bull market**. One in which prices drop is a **bear market**. Since 1926, stock prices had been rising steadily. Many people called it the Great Bull Market.

In the absence of strict regulation, professional brokers and investors became increasingly inventive in finding ways to keep the bull market roaring. They found that they could multiply their profits enormously through **leverage.** Financial leverage is meant to increase the earning power of one's investment.

For the individual investor, the most practical form of leverage is called buying on **margin**. Margin is a form of credit that the broker allows his client for the

BUYING ON MARGIN

Buying stocks on *margin* is a way of buying on credit. The margin is the market value of stock for which you pay cash. For example, buying at a 40 percent margin means you pay cash for 40 percent of the stock you buy and purchase the other 60 percent on credit from your broker. Buying on margin allows you to buy more stock for your money. If the price of the stock rises, your profits will multiply. But there is one big risk with buying on margin: if the stock price falls, your losses are multiplied.

Because of the risk, brokers set a margin limit. For example, a 40 percent margin limit means that at least 40 percent of your stock must be purchased with cash. To purchase stock on margin, you must have a margin account with a broker. This account is like a savings account. However, the value of a margin account is the total value of the stocks you buy with cash plus whatever cash you deposit in the account.

Your margin account is the broker's security against the money you borrow to buy additional stocks. The value of the account must stay above the margin limit. As long as the value of the stocks in your margin account rise, there is no problem. But if their prices fall, the value of your margin account falls, too. If it drops below the margin limit, you will receive a *margin call* from the broker. When this happens, you must put more cash in the account or sell enough stock to bring your margin above the limit.

purpose of buying stocks. In the 1920s, brokers often allowed investors as low as 10 percent margin, requiring the investor to pay cash for only about 10 percent of the stock he or she purchased. The rest of the stock would be bought by the broker. This enabled investors to purchase up to ten times more stock with the cash they had available.

As long as the value of these stocks increased, buying on margin was great for investors and brokers alike. Investors' profits were multiplied, and brokers received a **commission**, or percentage of every sale. More importantly, brokers encouraged clients to buy on margin because they wanted the bull market to continue. A large volume of stock purchases helped spur the bull market.

To the small investor, buying on margin was like applying the "buy now, pay later" idea to their investments. Many Wall Street investment companies even used that idea in their advertisements. They placed ads in newspapers and magazines depicting bank managers as friendly fellows ready with unlimited cash and brokers ready to "help you make your fortune." The ads worked, and money poured into Wall Street. Every day new investment trust companies opened to handle the growing market of investors.

For some small investors, the temptation of the stock market was simply too great to resist. With the opportunity to make a fortune practically guaranteed by many investment companies, they invested whatever money they could get their hands on—even if it wasn't *exactly* theirs. For example, a group of tellers and officers of the Union Industrial Bank, a local bank in Flint, Michigan, agreed on a plan to falsify the bank's books and "borrow" cash from the bank.

Frank Montague, one of the bank's vice-presidents, was a little nervous about the plan. However, others in the group included his trusted friend and fellow church member, Milton Pollock, and Robert Brown, son of the bank's president. They assured Montague that they were not stealing. They were merely "borrowing from the bank without approval." Montague went along with the idea, and as the group began to realize profits in the booming market and paid back some of its borrowings, Montague continued to participate.

When news reached the gentlemen of Union Industrial Bank in March 1929 that RCA was "taking off," they met to discuss whether or not to "borrow" more bank funds. Montague urged caution. It was better, he thought, to wait and see what developed in the next few days. The others agreed. A week later, with RCA selling at 101, they decided it was time to buy in.

By then, Meehan's pool was already taking its profits and selling thousands of shares. As sell offers outnumbered buy offers, the price of the stock continued to fall. Five days later, the men of Flint decided it was time to cut their losses and get out. RCA shares were selling for 87¼, and Montague and his friends had lost about $75,000 of the bank's money.

The case in Flint was not unique. The promise of easy wealth lured bank officials in banks throughout the country. Some did not have to **embezzle** in order to profit from bank funds. Charles Mitchell, the highly respected chairman of National City Bank, knew that by law his bank could not lend money to buy shares in the bank. So in 1928, Mitchell withdrew his bank from the market.

Then he formed an **affiliate**, the National City Company, of which he was also the chairman. This company was nothing more than a **holding company**, created for the purpose of speculating on the stock market. For Mitchell and his associates, the holding company worked like this: Borrowing from National City *Bank*, they invested heavily in National City *Company*. Between January 1928 and March 1929, Mitchell and his associates had been able to drive the value of a single share in National City Company from $785 to an astounding $2,000 a share.

By March 1929, rising stock prices seemed to be based more on the fictions created by an unregulated market than by the reality of increased production

H-HOLD YOUR BREATH! —SHE'S A-RUNNIN'!

OCCASIONAL PROSPERITY

PUBLIC

BUSINESS MAN

INDUSTRIAL ST.

A SCORE OF YEARS AGO THE OLD-FASHIONED BUSINESS MAN WAS DELIGHTED WITH OCCASIONAL PROSPERITY

TO-DAY, PROSPERITY IS ACCEPTED AS A PERMANENT THING BY THE MODERN BUSINESS MAN

HOME, JAMES!

PUBLIC

BUSINESS MAN

PERMANENT PROSPERITY

INDUSTRIAL BLVD.

ANOTHER MODERN IMPROVEMENT
—Orr in the Chicago *Tribune.*

This 1929 cartoon shows the optimism of those who believed the country had entered the age of "permanent prosperity."

THE HOLDING COMPANY

The business of some corporations is not to sell a product or service, but to buy and manage other companies that do. Such a corporation is called a ***holding company***. Hundreds of these companies were started in the 1920s. Some of them provided valuable capital and management to help smaller companies grow. Others, however, were started as a way to raise money for the purpose of speculating on the stock market. Promising their investors big profits, these companies took the capital from the sales of their stock and reinvested it in other companies.

and sales. Many financial experts, including Alexander Noyes, financial editor of *The New York Times*, warned the nation against unrealistic speculation. Paul Warburg of the International Acceptance Bank went so far as to call on President Hoover to help restrain "the present orgy of unrestrained speculation." Part of the problem, as Warburg saw it, was that banks were making it too easy to borrow money for speculation.

Warburg called for the **Federal Reserve Board**, which generally controlled the nation's **interest rates**, to raise the **rediscount rate**. This is the rate at which banks could borrow money from the Federal Reserve Bank. Much of the money was then loaned to brokers at a higher interest rate, to buy stocks on margin. A higher rediscount rate would discourage brokers from offering their clients such high margins. Warburg predicted that if the Federal Reserve Board did not act, the stock market would undergo a disastrous collapse that "would bring about a general depression involving the entire country."

The members of the Federal Reserve Board were in an awkward position. It was becoming obvious that stocks in many companies were overvalued. Yet to reverse the trend of rising stock prices would be painful for many investors. Falling stock prices could wipe out the savings of rich and poor alike.

Investors who had bought stock on margin were in particular danger. As long as stock prices rose, these investors multiplied their profits greatly. But when prices dropped, their losses were also multiplied. Worse yet, there was a limit on how much they could owe their brokers. As soon as they passed that limit, they had to pay the broker more cash or sell some of their stock. A rapid drop in the stock market could ruin many of these investors.

In March 1929, the members of the Federal Reserve Board decided on a cautious approach, one they hoped would deflate the speculation bubble gradually. The board issued instructions to banks to reduce the amount of money available for speculation. The instructions were advisory only and carried no penalties for those who disregarded them.

The effect on the stock market was more dramatic than the Federal Reserve Board had anticipated. On Tuesday, March 26, news of the "Fed's" move rang like a shot through financial circles. It was interpreted as a signal that stock market prices were too high. Many bankers reacted by raising the rates on broker's loans as high as 20 percent. Sell orders poured in at a record rate. Prices dropped dramatically.

Before the day was out, thousands of investors were receiving telegrams from their brokers. In stark contrast to previous, friendly communications from their brokers, "ready to help you make a fortune," these telegrams were terse: "SEND MORE MONEY PROMPTLY." Many investors had no money to send.

Selling stocks barely covered what they owed their brokers—and sometimes not even that. For many, March 26, 1929 brought an end to their dream of riches.

When William Durant heard the news of the stock market decline, he was furious. He decided to pay a visit to his old friend, Herbert Hoover, president of the United States. First, he did some research. He sent telegrams to executives of one hundred of America's most important companies. The telegram contained one question. Durant wanted to know if these executives believed, based on "present conditions and plans for the future," that the market price of their stock was too high. Of course, most executives wanted to see stock in their companies rise. Not surprisingly, the majority of them answered Durant's question, no. They did not believe that the market price in their stock was too high.

Armed with this "watertight" argument, Durant went to see President Hoover on April 4. He warned him that a major financial collapse was inevitable unless the Federal Reserve Board stopped its efforts to control brokerage loans and credit. He ended his argument with the words, "It's up to you now."

Meanwhile, Charles Mitchell, the chairman of the National City Bank, decided to take the situation into his own hands. Mitchell openly defied the Federal Reserve Board. He announced that his bank would continue to make brokerage loans with "no questions asked." He blamed the board for the "unnecessary panic" caused by the cutback in loans it had demanded.

As soon as Mitchell held a press conference on Wednesday, March 27, promising to continue supporting spec-ulators on the stock market, the gloom lifted from Wall Street. Other banks soon followed suit. In defiance of the Federal Reserve Board, they lowered brokers' loans. For the time being, the "bulls" on Wall Street, who wanted stock prices to continue rising, had overpowered the Federal Reserve Board. Brokers went back to borrowing, investors went back to buying on margin, and the Great Bull Market went raging on.

Three
The Crash

Henry Ford

William Durant was not the only businessman to visit President Hoover in the spring of 1929. On May 24, Henry Ford paid his own visit to the president, and following his meeting with Hoover, Ford held a press conference. Asked his opinion about the current stock market, Ford amazed the reporters by answering, "I don't know a thing about it. I never looked at a stock quotation in my life."

His admission notwithstanding, Ford went on to blast "the two-faced jokers from Wall Street." He also announced his plans for building a new plant in Portugal, another in Brazil, and a third in Russia. He pointed out that even though it was not a public corporation, Ford Motor Company was still one of the world's largest and most powerful companies. It was producing 8,000 cars a day and had a cash balance of almost $1 billion.

Ford's outlook on the nation's prosperity had also brightened. Perhaps because 1929 had been a successful year for his company, he seemed to dismiss, at least for the moment, his fears of Wall Street speculators. On his trip to Washington, he had seen signs of prosperity. He told reporters:

We have seen many new houses. With new paint on them. Paint is a good sign of prosperity. For both the people and the paint concerns.

Ford's oldest son, Edsel, was not as optimistic as his father. In part, he was worried simply because his father was not. Increasingly, it was Edsel who was managing the business of Ford Motor Company. Unlike his father, Edsel followed the activities of the stock market closely, and he did not share Henry's blind hatred of Wall Street. He wished his father would recognize that Ford Motor Company was not an isolated giant. Edsel Ford realized that, like it or not, the stock market did affect the Ford Motor Company. If people made profits from the stock market, Ford would sell more cars. If prices on the stock market dropped, Ford's sales would also drop.

Stubborn though he may have been, Henry Ford was finding it impossible to ignore the stock market. In fact, though he did not like to publicize it, Ford had already conceded the need to raise public capital. To finance his ambitious world-wide expansion, Ford had established a public corporation in England. So, although no shares in the Ford Motor Company could be purchased in the United States, stock in the Ford Motor Company of England was traded publicly in that country.

When Henry Ford learned that American investors had purchased five times more shares of this company than British investors, he was furious. He announced to the press that he intended to restrict the sale of Ford shares to no more than one or two per purchaser. No one asked him how he intended to do this. But his belief that he could was further proof that he misunderstood the point Edsel had been trying to make: Even the powerful Ford Motor Company was not independent from stock market activity. This fact would become increasingly true in the months and years ahead.

READING THE NEWSPAPER STOCK TABLES

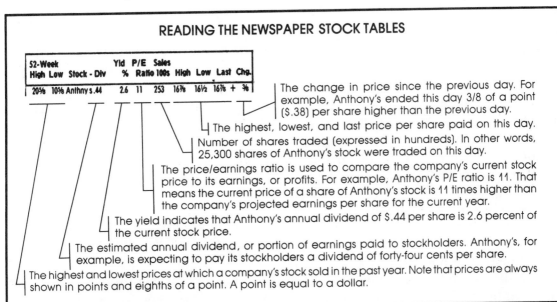

52-Week High Low	Stock - Div	Yld %	P/E Ratio	Sales 100s	High	Low	Last	Chg.
20⅝ 10⅝	Anthnys .44	2.6	11	253	16⅞	16½	16⅞	+ ⅜

The change in price since the previous day. For example, Anthony's ended this day 3/8 of a point ($.38) per share higher than the previous day.

The highest, lowest, and last price per share paid on this day.

Number of shares traded (expressed in hundreds). In other words, 25,300 shares of Anthony's stock were traded on this day.

The price/earnings ratio is used to compare the company's current stock price to its earnings, or profits. For example, Anthony's P/E ratio is 11. That means the current price of a share of Anthony's stock is 11 times higher than the company's projected earnings per share for the current year.

The yield indicates that Anthony's annual dividend of $.44 per share is 2.6 percent of the current stock price.

The estimated annual dividend, or portion of earnings paid to stockholders. Anthony's, for example, is expecting to pay its stockholders a dividend of forty-four cents per share.

The highest and lowest prices at which a company's stock sold in the past year. Note that prices are always shown in points and eighths of a point. A point is equal to a dollar.

THE CRYSTAL BALL APPROACH

In the 1920s most investors listened to financial experts and read financial reports before deciding what stocks to buy or sell. Some people, however, relied on more unusual advice. Astrologist Evangeline Adams became a national celebrity by advising the likes of actress Mary Pickford, steel tycoon Charles Schwab, and even the famous J.P. Morgan Sr.

Other investors relied on equally strange advice. One system that gained a following was based on the idea that no bull market would collapse in a month that did not have an 'R' in its name. Another was based on sunspots, and a third on a complicated decoding of the dialogue in popular comic strips. Finally, there was the much heralded "oyster theory." According to this theory, which thousands of investors apparently believed, the stock market would peak during the oyster season.

After its sudden decline in March, the stock market had rebounded. Not only did stocks return to their March highs, they surpassed them. The optimism of Wall Street speculators and the willingness of most banks to continue to make loans for stock purchases kept the bull market running strong throughout the summer.

Oddly, none of the problems that had led to the March decline had been addressed. People continued to borrow heavily to finance stock purchases, and stocks remained overvalued. For reasons not directly related to the stock market, the American economy was becoming sluggish. Consumers were buying fewer goods, which meant that manufacturers cut back on production—and on employment.

None of this had an immediate effect on Wall Street. Banking leaders like Charles Mitchell, industrialists like John Raskob, and investors like William Durant insisted that stock prices could continue to increase. Raskob claimed that the market could climb for another twenty years:

By 1949, when I might well be dead and forgotten but for the Empire State Building, people will still be playing the bull market.

On Tuesday, August 20, 1929, stocks had risen briskly. The **Dow Jones industrial average** reached an all-time high of 331 points. *The Wall Street Journal* reported what most speculators were waiting to hear:

This reestablishes the major upward trend. The outlook for the fall months seems brighter than at any time in recent years.

On Labor Day, another authority claimed, "The Dow Jones could climb to heaven!" This authority was astrologist Evangeline Adams, America's most famous fortune teller. Though her predictions were not as scientific as those made by Wall Street bankers, thousands of clients consulted Adams before placing their buy and sell orders on the stock market.

The next day, September 3, 1929, the crowds of amateur and small investors began forming on Wall Street earlier than usual. At 7:00 A.M., people had begun arriving by bus and subway. They came from the Midwest, from the deep South, even from Canada. There were lumberjacks from Montana, cowboys from Texas, farmers from California, and shopkeepers from Pennsylvania, all eager to get the right tip or be at the right place when a stock began to rise.

When Charles Mitchell, the banker who had defied the Federal Reserve Board, appeared on the street, he was greeted as if he were a war hero. People clapped and cheered. Some reached out to try to touch him. Others asked for market tips. Beaming, Mitchell advised

them to put their trust in National City Company.

By the time trading began on the stock exchange floor, the crowd outside and in the visitors' gallery was estimated at ten thousand people. They had all come to witness the market advance that so many had predicted. They were not disappointed. By the time the day ended, exhausted brokers had traded a record 4,438,910 shares. The Dow Jones industrial average had reached a record 381. Evangeline Adams' prediction seemed to be coming true.

Two days later, on Thursday, September 5, economist Roger Babson was scheduled to address the annual National Business Conference in Boston. It was a slow news day, and many reporters were on hand for Babson's speech. His words punctured the euphoria of the past few business days like a needle in a balloon:

Sooner or later a crash is coming which will take in the leading stocks and cause a decline of from sixty to eighty points in the Dow Jones barometer.

THE DOW JONES INDUSTRIAL AVERAGE

The Dow Jones industrial average is the most popular indicator of the overall direction of the whole stock market from day to day. It is an average based on the stock prices of thirty leading companies listed on the New York Stock Exchange. The high mark of the Dow Jones industrial average before the Crash of 1929 was 353 points, reached on October 10, 1929. After the crash, the Dow Jones fell to its lowest point, 41, on July 8, 1933. The 1929 high of 353 was not reached again until 1954.

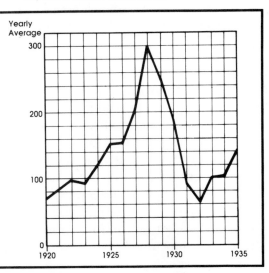

The next day, Babson's message made headlines in most of the nation's newspapers. *The New York Times* headline read:

"ECONOMIST PREDICTS 60 TO 80 POINTS STOCKMARKET CRASH."

In the days following Babson's speech, the stock market lost much of the gain it had made on September 3. But again, backed by optimistic speculators, it rallied. On October 1, John Raskob showed his confidence in the economy by unveiling his plan to begin construction of the Empire State Building. He insipired speculators with his typical flair:

> *In years to come, stocks will sell for ten times their present price, and brokers' loans will be billions more than they are now....*
> *Powerful factors are now giving unfavorable attention to Wall Street. These factors must be met face on. In a healthy market we prosper; in a sick market we suffer.*

Spurred on by the enthusiasm of Raskob and others, investors managed to sustain stock market prices through much of September. But the economic news was not encouraging. Steel and auto production were down. Unemployment was up. Also up was the amount of money being loaned to brokers for financing margin purchases.

Finally, after months of delay, the Federal Reserve Board raised the rediscount interest rate from 5 percent to 6 percent. By raising the rediscount rate, the board hoped to discourage speculation on the stock market once and for all. The plan worked. Almost immediately,

most banks raised their brokers' loans. The high interest discouraged brokers from allowing clients to buy stocks on margin.

With margins being scaled back, the stock market was erratic during the month of October. One day prices would drop drastically, only to be rallied the next by encouragement from the big investors. "Organized support," the kind of trade pool strategy used by Michael Meehan and others, became a favorite phrase in financial circles. Whenever a serious fall seemed inevitable, organized support would rescue the sagging market with a rush of buy orders.

Besides using their capital to stabilize the market, important finance companies, such as J.P. Morgan and Company, openly defied the Federal Reserve Board. Thomas Lamont,

Morgan's chief financial spokesman, sent a twenty-page report to President Hoover. In it, he denied that the current economic signs were bad:

The future appears brilliant. It is this future which the stock market has been discounting...we have the greatest and soundest prosperity, and the best material prospects of any country in the world. Our national resources, our selected population, our great domestic market, our efficiency and our capital supplies make our securities the most desirable in the world....Corrective action on the part of public authorities or individuals need not at this time be comtemplated.

In his eloquent style, Lamont was urging President Hoover to force the Federal Reserve Board to back off. "Don't rock the boat," he seemed to be saying, "and the economy will take care of itself."

It was too late; the boat had already been rocked—not only by the Federal Reserve Board, but by a combination of factors. On Wednesday, October 23, prices on the New York Stock Exchange began to fall once again.

At 6:30 A.M., Thursday, October 24, Frank Montague awoke at his home in Flint, Michigan. The officer of the Union Industrial Bank could not go back to sleep. The day before, Montague and his co-conspirators at the bank had placed a large sum of "borrowed funds" on General Motors stock. By the end of the day, GM had fallen twenty dollars a share.

"No, I have to stay here and work. I'm unloading copper."

The New Yorker

The "good life," as enjoyed by a 1920s investor. Here, "unloading copper" means selling stock in a mining company.

While sipping his morning coffee and listening to the stock reports on the radio, Montague pondered his choices. He could go to the bank president and confess, or he could risk falling even deeper in debt to the bank. Montague loved his family. He knew they admired and trusted him. He could not bear the thought of the shock they would suffer if they knew what he had done. Desperately hoping for a miraculous surge in the stock market, Montague decided to plunge further into debt.

The news on the radio brightened his spirits. Wall Street sources were quoted as saying that once again, the market was about to receive "positive organized support." At about the same hour in New York City, the men behind this "positive organized support" were arriving at their offices.

Again a huge crowd gathered outside the stock exchange, but this time it was a quiet, tense crowd. A shoeshine man recalled the scene:

People just stood there, stopped talking, and looked towards the Stock Exchange. It was like the silence before the start of a big race.

As 10:00 A.M. approached, William Durant, Charles Mitchell, John Raskob, Thomas Lamont, and many other **financiers** positioned themselves near the tickers in their offices. On the stock exchange floor, Michael Meehan, Thomas Bragg, Brad Ellsworth, Ben Smith, and the other thirteen hundred brokers were poised, quietly awaiting the gong.

At three minutes after ten, one of them shouted, "She's trading big and brisk!" Sure enough, the market had

Crowds gathered outside the New Yc

opened with an upward surge. The calls to clerks came quickly now, as the market began what appeared to be another dramatic rebound.

Then, at 10:25, a huge block of General Motors stock was sold at a loss of $.80 a share. A few minutes later, Meehan picked up a phone. In a hysterical voice, the caller shrieked, "Sell GM at the going price." At that moment, the same request was being heard in brokerage houses across the nation.

By 11:30, the only word to describe the scene on the exchange floor was panic. Brokers ran, pushed, shoved, and

...tock Exchange on Black Thursday.

the clerk's voice.

In Flint, Michigan, it was mid-morning before Frank Montague heard any more news about the stock market. What he heard made him feel sick. General Motors had been hit hard again. Yet Montague did not yet know how bad it really was. By this time, the ticker tapes at the stock exchange were hopelessly behind. Operators could not type in the information fast enough. General Motors was already much lower than the ticker tape was reporting.

At noon, a hastily called meeting took place at the offices of J.P. Morgan and Company. It was attended by the presidents of New York's four largest banks. According to one reporter, the group assembled there "represented more than $6 billion of banking resources."

When the meeting broke up an hour later, Mitchell left the House of Morgan calm and relaxed. Just his appearance helped to ease the tension in the crowd outside the stock exchange. "It's going to be alright," people whispered.

Word spread that Mitchell and his colleagues had established a multi-million-dollar fund to steady the market. Early in the afternoon, one of the floor brokers for J.P. Morgan and Company walked directly to Post Two and asked what the last bid he had received for U.S. Steel was. "195," he was told.

The broker shouted loudly, "Ten thousand shares at 205." He had just raised the bid for U.S. Steel by ten dollars. Almost instantly, a cheer rose up from all sides. From that point in the day, prices stopped falling. A few stocks even gained a point or two. "Organized support" had saved the day again.

cursed as they tried to fill all their sell orders. Anyone who uttered the word "buy" was immediately swarmed by a mob of brokers. At Trading Post One, brokers were literally being pinned against the trading counter by the throng. At other posts, the scene was equally frenzied.

William Hut, a broker on the floor, recalls calling a clerk on the phone to get the latest price quotes. The clerk wailed, "I can't get them. I can't get any information! The whole place is falling apart!" It was not so much the words that startled Hut as the tone of despair in

The Dow Jones industrial average only showed a decline of 6.38 points, thanks to the end-of-the-day rally sparked by the banking group. But the small drop in the Dow was deceptive. It was based on dramatic increases in the few stocks the bankers' group had decided to support. Also, prices of many stocks had dropped so low before the bankers came to the rescue that thousands of people had to sell in order to cover their margin limits. In many cases, they did not even make enough from these sales to pay what they owed on margin. In a few short hours, thousands of people had lost not only their dream of fortune, but their life's savings.

Sell orders had come in so fast that a total of thirteen million shares were traded at the New York Stock Exchange that day. The volume of sales was so great that the ticker tapes could not keep up. This added to the panic, and it also cost many people dearly. Brokerage houses across America did not receive the news of the afternoon rally until after the market had closed. By that time, they had already sent telegrams to thousands of clients telling them to "Sell or send more money."

Ever since, Thursday, October 24, 1929 has been known as Black Thursday. As bad as things were, however, many people sensed a peculiar feeling of optimism. The market was reeling from a bad blow, but it had survived the knock-out punch. The prevailing attitude seemed to be that the worst was over. Even Alexander Noyes, the cautious financial editor of *The New York Times*, allowed a sense of optimism in the stories his paper ran. The next day's headlines read:

*WORST STOCK CRASH
STEMMED BY BANKS.*

*LEADERS CONFER, FIND
CONDITIONS SOUND.*

For most brokers, Thursday and Friday seemed like one long, continuous day. Many stayed at their offices overnight, sorting out piles of paperwork and figuring out their clients' accounts. When they appeared at the stock exchange for business on Friday morning, they were exhausted. Many had gone without sleep. Some had not even changed clothes.

Nevertheless, most approached the day with a determined optimism. They had weathered the storm, and they reasoned that conditions would begin to improve. Most expected the Federal Reserve Board to lower its rediscount rate so that brokers and investors would be encouraged to buy.

The members of the Federal Reserve Board met almost all day Friday. Some members believed that speculation had been satisfactorily controlled. They recommended lowering the rediscount rate back to 5 percent. Other members argued that the Dow Jones average had only declined six points, and that speculators had already tried to push stock

prices back up. The board adjourned Friday afternoon without any decision or any announcement to the public. Most people expected that its announcement would come Monday. Friday and Saturday were slow days on the market, ending in slight losses for most stocks.

Over the weekend, bankers and politicians did their best to assure the nation that Thursday's panic was a "technical" correction. In other words, prices of stocks that were overvalued were lowered to match realistic predictions of earnings and growth. Most importantly, they stressed that they expected the bull market to continue.

President Hoover declared his optimism:

*The fundamental business of the country, that is production and distribution of **commodities**, is on a sound and prosperous basis.*

Herbert Hoover

What no one seemed to realize was how fragile the economy was, or how it had been weakened by speculation. Most of the capital in the stock market was not going toward the fundamental business of production and distribution. Instead it was going to speculators who had set up elaborate chains of investment trust companies and holding companies, which produced nothing. Their only service was to drive the stocks of other companies higher than their real value.

No one could predict how seriously Thursday's panic had damaged the stock market until it reopened on Monday. Almost immediately, Thursday's scene was repeated. The volume of sales was not as high, but the losses were much greater. All day, prices continued to fall. By day's end, the Dow Jones average had dropped another thirty-eight points. The total value of stocks traded on the New York Stock Exchange dropped $14 billion.

Even worse, there were two signals that the crash was not over. First, the lowest prices of the day were recorded in the last few minutes of trading. There was no last minute upturn to show any promise of change. Secondly, there was no evidence of movement by the bankers' group that had rescued the market on Thursday. The great bulls had given up.

Tuesday, October 29, 1929, is the day most often cited as the "day of the crash." It was probably the worst day in the history of the stock market. Sixteen million shares were traded, and the Dow Jones dropped another thirty points. At this point, however, the events of the stock market were a foregone conclusion. Without "positive organized support" from bankers and big investors, there was little hope for a recovery.

Around the country, that reality was beginning to sink in. At 1:30 P.M. Tuesday, in Flint, Michigan, Frank Montague estimated that he and his co-workers owed the bank about $3 million. Seeing no other choice, he went to the president of the bank. As it turned out, Montague's estimate was a little low. All told, he and his fellow conspirators

BEARS WIN

In the language of the stock market, a bear is someone who expects stock prices to fall. Many shrewd bears made a lot of money during the crash using a technique called selling short.

Technically, selling short means selling stock before you actually own it. You can do this by temporarily borrowing the stock from a broker. Then, if you expect the price of that stock to drop, you can sell it before the price drops. After the price drops, you can buy the stock you owe the broker and return it. But since you are buying it at a cheaper price than what you sold it for, you make a profit.

Selling short is still legal today, although many restrictions apply. In 1929, few restrictions prevented a bear from profiting by selling short. Many bears who sold short during the crash made millions.

had lost $3,592,000 of the bank's money.

At least a million other Americans were immediately and directly affected by the crash. Some, like Frank Montague, were financially wiped out. Often the money they received for their stocks did not even pay what they owed their brokers.

One investor who had been hit particularly hard was James Riordan, the friend whom John Raskob had persuaded to begin speculating with Meehan's pool. A few days after the crash, Riordan, who was a widower, spoke with his two grown daughters on the telephone. The occasion was his younger daughter's nineteenth birthday. "If things are tight," she told him, he need not worry about giving her a gift.

At about 6:00 P.M. on Friday, November 8, 1929, James Riordan was sitting in his New York home. He placed a revolver to his head and pulled the trigger. Still conscious, he fell to the floor. Shortly before he died, he whispered to his butler, "What's going to happen to my girls?"

Riordan's suicide is the most famous one associated with the Crash of 1929. There were others, undoubtedly, although statistics show only a small increase in suicides in the days immediately following the crash. Most of the stories of investors leaping from windows and throwing themselves off of bridges are myths. Most of those who were hit hardest by the crash went on with their lives, although in many cases, their lives were drastically changed.

The week of the crash had been an exciting week for Henry Ford. But Ford's excitement had nothing to do with the stock market. While the rest of the nation was riveted to every report about the market, Ford hardly had time to give it a second thought. Indeed, one of the few distractions people around the country enjoyed during the week of crisis was the live radio coverage of the grand opening of Ford's American Village in Dearborn, Michigan.

President Hoover was on hand at the opening ceremony to light a fire in the hearth of Abraham Lincoln's courthouse. But the highlight of the event was the appearance of Thomas Edison, now a man of eighty-five, to re-enact his invention of the incandescent light bulb at the village's replica of the Edison laboratory.

The splendid new theme park was a smashing success. Even Henry Ford must have been satisfied with the number of reporters who flocked to Dearborn during the park's opening week. Edison's re-enactment was described live throughout the nation by NBC radio. "It is people like Thomas Edison, Orville and Wilbur Wright, and Henry Ford who have made this country great," concluded the radio broadcaster. In New York City, William Durant, John Raskob, James Riordan, Michael Meehan, and other important men of Wall Street took time to enjoy the broadcast.

Soon, however, news of the crash drew reporters away from Ford's American Village. Once again, Wall Street had stolen his spotlight, and Henry Ford finally realized that what his son Edsel had been saying was true: There was no escaping the influence of Wall Street.

In the following months, Ford

observed the effects of the crash on the country. President Hoover called on Henry Ford and other business leaders to help recharge the slumping economy. In response, Ford cut the price of all his cars as a "contribution to the continuation of good business." He also raised employee wages from $6.00 to $7.00 a day. The gesture cost him about $20 million, but it did little to stimulate the sagging economy. Still, Ford insisted that the economy would rebound quickly. Reporters were fond of quoting his famous line: "Today is better than yesterday."

But the American people had become skeptical. Like Ford, many who had not even invested in the stock market now found themselves hurt by the crash. One immediate consequence was the weakness of many banks. Those that had loaned large amounts to support margin buying and other stock market speculation were unable to collect on many of their loans. The brokers who had borrowed from them were bankrupt. In order to make these loans in the first place, the banks themselves had borrowed from Federal Reserve Banks. Repaying their debts left many banks short of cash.

Often, when nervous bank customers went to withdraw their savings, they were in for a surprise. The banks did not have enough cash. This triggered a banking crisis in the weeks following the crash. Customers rushed to their banks to withdraw their savings. In the streets, huge lines formed in front of banks as people waited to get inside.

Brown Brothers

Panicked customers flocked to banks to withdraw their savings.

Ironically, these demands for cash only made things worse for the bank customers. If people had not panicked and withdrawn their money, most banks could have met their debts. As it was, thousands of banks declared bankruptcy, and the savings accounts of their loyal customers were wiped out.

The weakness in the economy, combined with the distrust of bankers and brokers, caused the stock market to fall steadily for the next two years. Stock prices were a far cry from the optimistic forecasts of the Great Bull Market. In 1929, the value of all stock listed with the New York Stock Exchange was $90 billion. By 1932, it had fallen to $16 billion.

This decline paralleled the drop in individual stocks. U.S. Steel dropped from a 1929 high of 262 to a low of 21. General Motors dropped from 92 to 7. RCA, one of the glamour stocks of the era, fell from 115 to 3. The Dow Jones average had reached a high of 386 in 1929. In 1932, it reached a low of 41.

THE NEW DEAL

By 1932, with the country deep in depression, President Hoover had become quite unpopular. He lost the presidential election that year to Franklin Roosevelt. Under Roosevelt's leadership, the Democratic party promised the American people a "new deal." They enacted laws such as the Securities Act of 1933 and Securities and Exchange Act of 1934 to restrain the financially powerful. They established a number of federal agencies like the **WPA**, or Works Progress Administration, to help provide jobs and relief for the nation's poor. Roosevelt's administration became known as the New Deal.

As stock prices dropped, so did consumer demands for goods. With little demand to meet, industrial production declined, and unemployment rose. The United States had entered what was to become the longest and most severe depression in its history.

By March 4, 1933, when Franklin Delano Roosevelt was inaugurated as the thirty-second president of the United States, the country had witnessed the

Franklin Roosevelt

could afford to buy new cars. Across the nation cars stood idle because their owners could not even afford to run them.

While almost all businesses were affected by the crash, small businesses suffered most. Without the capital resources to see them through, they could not survive long without profits. Many of these small businessmen, along with unemployed people in cities across the country, tried to make a living by selling fruits and vegetables. On the streets of America's cities, large numbers of people opened little stands where they could sell homegrown apples, homemade neckties, or offer a five-cent shoeshine.

failure of over six thousand banks, the *foreclosure* of half a million home loans, and the loss of thousands of family farms. Twenty-five percent of America's work force was unemployed. Many local governments were bankrupt. While receiving less income from taxes, they ran out of money trying to provide relief for the jobless and homeless of their cities.

The Ford Motor Company struggled to survive during the thirties. Few people

In most cities, long lines became a common sight. Every job opening attracted long lines of job hunters. Temporary "soup kitchens" and relief missions attracted lines of hungry and homeless people. In the twenties, the homeless aided by such missions had been mostly alcoholics, people with mental disorders, or fugitives from the law. During the thirties, nearly as many of the homeless were economic victims of the depression, people who had lost everything.

Many of the jobless took to the road. They followed rumors of jobs around the country. They worked on farms during harvest seasons. Hitching rides on the highways or riding in empty freight cars, they swelled the population of "hobo jungles" on the outskirts of many cities. Often the hobos located near city dumps, where they could build shacks out of tin, cardboard, and scraps of wood. These temporary communities became known as "Hoovervilles," alluding to President Hoover's inability to solve the unemployment crisis.

Not everyone suffered during the Great Depression. The unemployment rate was high, but 75 percent of American workers kept their jobs. Most of them had to tolerate lower wages than they had earned during the twenties, but many were actually better off. The depression had caused a significant reduction in prices. A brand new Model A Ford cost $500 in 1929, while the 1934 model went for about $400. Food, clothing, appliances, and property all cost less.

Technology did not stand still during the thirties, either. Advances in aircraft made transcontinental flights faster and more comfortable. Improvements in automobiles made car travel more reliable, while new highways seemed to bring America's cities closer together. And new skyscrapers began to appear on the the skylines of these cities.

The man who financed the Empire State Building, John J. Raskob, reportedly lost millions in the crash. Yet, like other wealthy investors, his fortune was not depleted. Raskob decided that his dream of building the 102-story Empire State Building could be a symbol of hope in a troubled time. On St. Patrick's Day, March 17, 1930, the first steel piers were sunk into position to support the 365,000 tons of steel, stone, concrete, and glass. Raskob had observation stands erected around the construction site. Every day, thousands of visitors would come to watch the project take shape. For those who could not witness it personally, radio reports and movie newsreels kept them abreast of the building's progress. On May 1, 1931, President Hoover officially opened it. John Raskob told anyone who would

listen that his Empire State Building was proof that "the good times" would return. They were a long time in coming.

Two other powerful figures on Wall Street, Michael Meehan and J.P. Morgan Jr., son of the famous entrepreneur, also survived the crash with their fortunes intact. The same could not be said for their reputations. During the thirties, the image of brokers and bankers in the United States underwent a dramatic change. In the twenties they were identified as friends of the common people, ready to help people make their fortunes. In the thirties they were seen as little better than crooks who benefited from the misfortunes of others.

Charles Mitchell, the chairman of National City Bank, was one banker who fit this perception best. Mitchell had blatantly defied the law in creating the National City Company as an investment and holding company for the bank. He, like most of the company's clients, had purchased outrageously overvalued stock on margin. The margin accounts were financed by National City Bank.

THE EMPIRE STATE BUILDING

As the Empire State Building rose, it helped raise the spirits of people around the country, and it provided at least a small boost to the economy. The building required 57,000 tons of steel, and another 300,000 tons of stone, concrete, and glass. During the year it was built, it provided 3,000 jobs.

When it was finished in 1931, the Empire State Building stood 102 stories high and rose 1,250 feet in the air. For more than 30 years it was the tallest building in the world.

He lost about $40 million. Several brokerage houses sued him for unpaid commissions.

In 1930, Durant had one final flicker of bullishness left. He had set aside 187,000 shares of General Motors in a trust fund for his wife, Catherine. Now he took them, with her permission, and sold them to invest in companies he believed would make a fast recovery. Durant's magic touch had left him. The recovery never came, and the 187,000 shares of GM, which would have been worth a small fortune ten years later, were gone.

In those ten years, William Durant tried one scheme after another to build another empire. He took one last stab at the auto industry, but his Durant Motor Car Company went bankrupt in 1933. Three years later, Durant himself filed for bankruptcy. His debts totalled approximately $1 million. He listed his total **assets** as "clothing, valued at $250."

Next, Durant opened a lunchroom restaurant in New Jersey. It failed. In 1940, he opened a bowling alley. Almost eighty at the time, he spoke of creating a chain of bowling alleys and of other ambitious ventures. They never materialized.

In 1942, Durant suffered a severe stroke. Confined to a wheelchair, he lived another five years. His wife Catherine paid for their medical bills and living expenses by selling off her jewelry, piece by piece. Michael Meehan, John Raskob, Walter Chrysler, and other old friends, still millionaires, slipped him handouts when they came to visit. In a meager New York apartment, on March 18, 1947, William Durant, the founder of General Motors, died at eighty-five.

As a result of the crash, Mitchell lost not only his fortune, but his position with the bank. He was also tried in federal court for tax evasion. By 1933, Mitchell was reportedly $12 million in debt. However, he was acquitted of all criminal charges and started over again in the investment business. Eventually, Mitchell became chairman of Blythe & Company, a respected investment firm, and he prospered once again.

The wrongdoing of Frank Montague and eight other officers and tellers with Union Industrial Bank in Flint, Michigan, was easier to prove. Unlike Charles Mitchell, these men had been unable to disguise their illegal activities. On December 16, 1929, the Flint bankers pleaded guilty to charges of embezzlement. Frank Montague was sentenced to 3½ years in prison. His co-conspirator, Robert Brown, son of the bank's president, was sentenced to six months.

The most vocal and adamant of the bulls on Wall Street in 1929 had been William Durant. Durant stayed in the dying bull market until the bitter end.

Five
Could It Happen Again?

Slowly, the nation pulled itself out of the Great Depression. Most economists agree that the event most responsible for ending the depression was World War II. As young men enlisted in the armed forces, the unemployment rate dropped dramatically. The demand for weapons, tanks, aircraft, ammunition, and supplies brought much needed work to American factories. This broke the cycle of depression.

While they agree about how it ended, economists are not as certain why the Great Depression began. Some claim that the Crash of 1929 caused the depression. Others maintain that the depression caused the crash. These economists point out that production had already begun to decline and unemployment was going up before the crash occurred.

On the other hand, while a drop in production and employment usually signals a **recession**, it has never, before or since, caused such a serious setback as the Great Depression. One of the main differences between previous recessions and the Great Depression is the role played by the stock market. It would not be accurate to say that the crash alone caused the Great Depression, but there is little doubt that it made the depression much worse.

The Crash of 1929 and the depression that followed are the greatest financial crises in American history. They both came on the heels of the new era in American finance, the era of the public corporation. One explanation for the crash and the depression is that people were not ready for this new era or the changes it brought. The banking system was not ready, the business leaders were not ready, and the American government was not ready to handle the power of a corporate economy. The people of the 1920s saw the promise of a new economic era, but they did not see the risks—at least not in time.

What were these risks? (1) The stock market was unregulated, which permitted people to manipulate huge amounts of money to their own advantage and to the disadvantage of others. (2) The banking structure was weak. (3) People had little understanding of a corporate economy. (4) Technology, especially in the communications industry, was inadequate for keeping up with

Just around the corner

The New Yorker

Every time stock prices seemed to be on their way back up, the stock market would take another dive.

Visitors to the New York Stock Exchange in 1940.

the rapid exchange of huge sums of money. And (5), the greatest risk of all, people were greedy.

In 1929, there was little government control of the stock market. Each stock exchange was self-regulating. In other words, the members of the exchange agreed to the rules of operation and had their own officers to enforce them. Breaking the rules of the exchange was not a legal offense. Looking back on this period, William O. Douglas, Supreme Court justice during the Roosevelt era, characterized American stock exchanges as "private clubs, inappropriate for a business so vested with public interest."

The members of the New York Stock Exchange had incredible freedom to manipulate prices and control credit. Trade pools, such as those organized by Michael Meehan, could create an artificial stock demand. Its participants could make huge profits and leave the unsuspecting public holding highly overvalued stock.

At the same time, brokers were free to set their own margin limits. Most brokers had a great deal to gain financially from the bull market and thought the best way to keep it going was to keep offering credit. That way, investors would continue to buy more and more stock, and the demand would keep pushing prices up. Besides buying on margin, big investors created mazes of investment companies and holding companies to multiply their profits. The problem with these schemes is that while they create profit on paper, they actually take investment money away from the companies that manufacture goods, employ workers, and sell products.

The second risk of the new era was that banks were poorly prepared for the widespread use of credit. As more and more investors borrowed to get in on "once-in-a-lifetime" stock opportunities, the banks followed no uniform policies to control lending. Again, government regulation was inadequate. The Federal Reserve Board and Federal Reserve banks had little authority to coordinate banking practices. Even when the Federal Reserve Board tried to regulate lending, independent banks openly refused to cooperate.

While the economy was shifting into a new era, the banking system remained in the old era. Although national and international corporations were increasing in both number and size, most of the nation's banks were small, independent, and privately owned. Immediately after the crash, nervous depositors ran to their local banks and withdrew their savings. Many banks did not have the funds to meet these demands. As soon as news spread that one bank had failed, panic

set in. Other people went to their banks and demanded their money, then those banks failed, and the panic spread. Once the domino effect started, there was no way to stop it.

The third risk of the new era, inadequate knowledge of finance and economics, was demonstrated by William Durant's "survey" of corporate executives. Durant believed, based on a yes or no answer to a single, highly subjective question, he had adequate proof that the nation's stocks were not overvalued. Armed with nothing more than a company executive's assurance that his company's stocks were sound, Durant sought to convince the president of the United States that stock prices were not too high.

Thomas Lamont, the financial expert with J.P. Morgan and Company, the world's most prestigious finance company, was more thorough in the report he sent to President Hoover. However, his conclusion was the same as Durant's, and it came just two days before Black Thursday.

The fact is, neither Durant, Lamont, nor anyone else in the country had a very complete picture of the economy. They did very little analysis of economic data. No one bothered to consider the combined effects of employment rates, production levels, interest rates, **inflation** rates, imports, exports, or foreign investment on the stock market. For the most part, investors in the 1920s looked at two factors: steel production and automobile sales. If these were up, it meant the economy was sound. If they were down, there was usually some rational explanation which implied that the economy was still sound.

In 1929, a busy day at the New York Stock Exchange meant trading two or three million shares of stock. When the panic set in on Black Thursday, almost 13 million shares were sold. On the following Tuesday, October 29, 16 million more shares were traded. On both days, the ticker tapes could not keep up with this frenzied pace. Price quotations fell nearly three hours behind the trading activity. In a market where prices were falling rapidly, many investors lost a great deal of money by not having current price information.

This was especially true on the afternoon of Black Thursday. Brokerage houses around the country were unaware that the bankers' group had moved in to support stock prices at the New York Stock Exchange. These houses mistakenly demanded that many clients sell stock to stay within their margin limits. They unnecessarily added to the panic and cost some people their life's savings.

Finally, the greatest risk of the new era was that greed consumed even the best of people. When the bull market began early in the 1920s, most stocks were sound investments. Their value was below the potential value of the company's assets and earnings.

Somewhere along the way, however, the reason for buying stock changed. Those who had made a fortune effortlessly in the stock market were worshipped. What people were buying and selling was no longer shares in a company, but dreams of an overnight fortune. As long as enough people remained convinced that instant wealth was possible, the bull market continued. As prices rose, people who bought stocks began paying a higher price for their dreams. But they remained convinced that market prices would continue to climb.

This attitude, more than anything else, ultimately led to the Crash of 1929. Of course, speculators had been assured regularly that the economy was sound and that stocks were not overvalued. But there were also warnings by respected economists that the bull market could not go on indefinitely. Those who continued to buy stocks did so because they wanted to believe they could get

THE STOCK MARKET THEN AND NOW

There is no way to guarantee that another crash like the one in 1929 will not happen, or that such a crash will not lead to another Great Depression. But many steps have been taken to try to keep this from happening. As a result, today's stock market is much different from the stock market of 1929.

Government Regulations

Then: Stock exchanges were self-regulated. Since government control of the stock market was so loose, it was easy for brokers and big investors to manipulate stock prices unfairly.

Credit Controls

Then: Brokers decided what margin limits to offer their clients. Many investors had margin limits as low as 10 percent. Ninety percent of the money they invested in the stock market was borrowed.

Volume of Trades

Then: A busy day of trading on the New York Stock Exchange in 1929 meant that about one or two million shares were traded. The thirteen million traded on Black Thursday and the sixteen million traded on the following Tuesday shattered all records.

Communications

Then: The ticker tape system could not keep up with the volume of trade on days like Black Thursday and the following Tuesday. This added to the panic because brokers and investors did not know what the latest stock prices were.

rich. As soon as they began to doubt this belief, the dream became a nightmare.

Since the Great Depression, people have wondered whether it could happen again. The only thing we know for certain is that we are now much better prepared for the risks of a corporate economy than were the people of the 1920s.

For one thing, the stock market is

and Exchange Commission. The SEC is in charge of maintaining a stock market free of price manipulation, speculation, and other unfair practices. All corporations that issue **securities**, or stocks and **bonds**, must be registered and reviewed by the SEC. These corporations must be businesses operating for the purpose of selling a product or service. Thus many types of holding companies popular in the 1920s are now illegal.

The SEC also disallows trade pools of any kind. In fact, "insider trading" is now against the law. A broker cannot rely on any information for completing or recommending a stock transaction unless that information is available to the general public.

The Securities Exchange Act also gives the Federal Reserve Board legal authority to regulate the use of credit for stock purchases. The board sets uniform margin requirements. It determines the maximum percentage of an investor's securities that can be bought on margin. The board has the power to raise the margin percentage to encourage investment, or lower it to curb speculation.

Now: The SEC carefully regulates the trading of stocks so that no one can manipulate prices or take advantage of private information.

Now: The Federal Reserve Board has the authority to set the minimum margin limits. It can lower this limit to encourage people to buy stock or raise it to discourage excessive speculation.

Now: The volume of trade at the New York Stock Exchange has increased astronomically. The average number of shares traded per day is now more than fifty million.

Now: The ticker tape system has been replaced by a computer system that instantly records and reports every transaction. It is estimated that this system can keep up with as many as 300 million shares a day.

now more carefully regulated. The Crash of 1929 prompted Congress to investigate its causes. As a result of that investigation, some important laws were passed. Two of these laws, the Securites Act of 1933 and the Securities Exchange Act of 1934, established the basis for regulating the stock market.

The Securities Exchange Act created the **SEC**, or the Securities

THE SEC

The SEC, Securities and Exchange Commission, was established by the Securities Exchange Act of 1934. Its purpose is to assure investors that the market for **securities**, including stocks and **bonds**, is a fair trading market. The commission is made up of five commissioners, each appointed by the president of the United States for a five-year term.

The SEC regulates stock exchanges and licenses stockbrokers. Any firm that issues securities must be registered with the SEC and regularly submit financial records to show that all their business dealings are legal.

Changes in the laws and banking practices have strengthened the nation's banks. The Banking Act of 1933 created the **FDIC**, the Federal Deposit Insurance Corporation. This federal agency guarantees deposits in banks. If a bank goes bankrupt, gets robbed, or if anything happens to its money, the federal government will pay the bank's depositors all or part of what the bank owes them. The FDIC helps prevent the kind of panic that occurred in 1929, when banks were unable to provide the cash demanded by nervous depositors.

Part of the reason for the panic in 1929, especially on Black Thursday, was that information about the stock market was communicated too slowly. The ticker tape system was only equipped to report trades of about ten million shares per day. Today the ticker system has been replaced by computers. In 1979, the facilities on the trading floor were completely overhauled. The oval trading booths were replaced by units equipped to carry a vast array of advanced communications systems. Now the stock exchange system is capable of recording the sale of more than 200 million shares a day.

While brokers, bankers, and government officials have all taken significant steps to reduce the possibility of another great crash, the one factor that no one can control is human greed. We now have the ability to control the kind of runaway speculation and panic that took place in 1929. But more than anything else, what kept the Great Bull Market alive in 1929 was greed. As long as people believed in the possibility of getting rich quickly, they kept paying more and more for stock. Can today's improved regulation, banking practices, information, and communication systems overcome greed and the illusion of riches?

On October 19, 1987, that question was put to the test. A bull market had been running almost uninterrupted for nearly four years. Rising stock prices reflected a growing economy. By 1987, the market seemed to be rising at its own pace. Millions of investors rushed to buy stock, hoping to make a quick profit. They leveraged their investment by buying on margin. Many economic analysts warned of the similarities between 1987 and 1929.

On Tuesday, October 19, 1987, the bull market came to a crashing halt. Sell orders began to pour in, and prices began to fall dramatically. All day, stocks lost ground. When the day began, the Dow Jones industrial average stood at 2247 points. By the end of trading, it was 1739, the largest one-day drop in the history of the stock market. The next day, prices continued to fall. Many wondered if another depression was just around the corner.

Unlike 1929, however, the 1987 decline in stock prices stopped after the second day. There was no panic. Stock prices stabilized and a gradual recovery began. For the time being, at least, the safeguards on the stock market had worked. It was very tempting for prominent political and financial leaders to point to the crash of 1987 as evidence that "our economy was basically sound." There is only one thing to worry about in those reassuring words. They have been used before—on the day before the worst financial crisis in American history.

Glossary

affiliate . . . . [uh-**FILL**-ee-it] A company legally connected to another.

annunciator board . . . [uh-**NUN**-see-ate-or] A display board mounted high on the wall of the trading room.

asset . . . . Anything owned that has value.

bear market . . . . A stock market trend of falling prices.

bond . . . . A note of debt for a loan from an investor to a corporation, which the corporation agrees to repay with interest.

broker . . . . A person who buys and sells stocks and bonds for others.

brokerage . . . . A company of brokers.

bull market . . . . A stock market trend of rising prices.

capital . . . . Money or property, especially that used in business to make more money.

commission . . . . A part of the money taken in from a sale which is used to pay the person making the sale.

commodity . . . . [cum-**MOD**-i-tee] Anything bought and sold.

corporation . . . . An organization, usually a business, that can legally own property and make contracts, as if it were a person.

dividend . . . . A payment made to a shareholder, representing his or her share of a company's profits.

**Dow Jones
industrial average** . . . . An average, computed daily, of the current prices of thirty selected industrial stocks traded on the New York Stock Exchange. Used to determine the state of the market.

embezzle . . . . [em-**BEZ**-ul] To steal money which has been placed in one's care.

entrepreneur . . . . [on-truh-pruh-**NOOR**] A person who organizes and manages a business undertaking, assuming the risk for the sake of the profit.

**Federal
Reserve Board** . . . . The board that supervises the federal banking system, which controls the supply of money and credit available to other banks.

FDIC . . . . Federal Deposit Insurance Corporation, an agency of the federal government, which guarantees deposits in a bank against theft or loss.

financier . . . . [fi-nan-**SEER**] A person who engages in financial operations on a large scale.

flapper . . . . A young woman considered to be bold and unconventional in the 1920s.

foreclosure . . . . [for-**CLO**-zher] The legal process that allows a bank or other creditor, which holds rights to a property through a loan agreement, to claim ownership because the terms of the agreement have not been upheld.

holding company . . . . . A company that sells no product or service but controls other companies that do.

inflation . . . . An increase in the amount of money in circulation. It makes money less valuable and brings prices up.

interest rate . . . . The percentage of a loan that a borrower agrees to pay a lender, in addition to repaying the amount borrowed.

investment . . . . Money put into business, real estate, stocks, bonds, etc. in order to earn a profit.

leverage . . . . The practice of using a small investment to control a much larger one.

margin . . . . The deposit paid by an investor when buying securities with funds loaned by a broker.

margin call . . . . A broker's demand for a client to deposit more cash in a margin account.

page . . . . A person who delivers messages and runs errands at the stock exchange.

pariah .... A person who is despised by others.

pneumatic tube ...... A tube using compressed air to transfer message containers from one end of the trading floor to the other.

point .... The measurement of stock value equal to one dollar.

prohibition .... The law forbidding people from buying or selling alcoholic beverages.

public corporation ... A corporation offering stock for sale to the public.

quotation .... The current stated price of a stock, bond, or commodity.

recession .... A period when business is poor; a mild economic depression.

rediscount rate .... The interest rate at which banks can borrow money from the Federal Reserve Bank for lending to others.

seat .... Membership to a stock exchange.

SEC .... Securities Exchange Commission. The agency of the federal government responsible for regulating the issuing and selling of stocks and bonds.

securities .... Any kind of ownership in a corporation, or representation of that ownership, such as stock certificates or bonds.

share .... A unit of stock in a corporation.

shareholder .... A person who owns stock in a corporation. A stockholder.

speakeasy .... A night club where alcoholic beverages are sold illegally.

speculate .... To buy commodities, such as stocks, with the expectation that they can be resold for profit.

stock exchange .... A place where stocks and bonds are bought and sold.

stock market .... The general business of buying and selling stocks and bonds.

stock .... Part ownership in a corporation.

stockholder .... A person who owns stock in a corporation. A shareholder.

ticker tape . . . . The paper tape used in a ticker for recording tele-graphed stock market prices.

ticker . . . . The machine that receives prices of securities by telegraph and prints them on paper.

trade . . . . To buy and sell stocks.

trading pool . . . . An organized group of investors who work together to influence stock prices.

trading post . . . . A structure on the trading floor where specific companies' stocks are traded.

WPA . . . . Works Progress Administration. An agency of the federal government during the 1930s, which pro-vided part-time jobs for the unemployed.

Wall Street . . . . A street in New York City; the financial center of the stock market.

Further Reading

THE STOCK MARKET AND THE CRASH OF 1929

Axon, Gordon V. *The Stock Market Crash of 1929*. New York: Mason/Charter Publishers, 1974.

Hiebert, Ray Elden. *The Stock Market Crash, 1929: Panic on Wall Street Ends the Jazz Age*. New York: Franklin Watts, 1970.

Little, Jeffrey B. and Lucien Rhodes. *Understanding Wall Street*. 2d ed. Blue Ridge Summit, Penn.: Liberty House, 1987.

Rosenblum, Marc. *The Stock Market*. Minneapolis: Lerner Publications, 1970.

Sterling, Dorothy. *Wall Street: The Story of the Stock Exchange*. Garden City, N.Y.: Doubleday, 1955.

Thomas, Gordon and Max Morgan-Witts. *The Day the Bubble Burst*. Garden City, N.Y.: Doubleday, 1968.

THE TWENTIES

Giles, Carl H. *1927: The Picture Story of a Wonderful Year*. New York: Arlington House, 1971.

Goodman, Paul and Frank Otto Gatell. *America in the Twenties*. New York: Holt Rinehart and Winston, 1972.

Jenkins, Alan. *The Twenties*. New York: Universe Books, 1974.

Mowry, George. *The Twenties: Fords, Flappers, and Fanatics*. Englewood Cliffs, N.J.: Prentice Hall, 1963.

Sloat, Warren. *1929: America Before the Crash*. New York: Macmillan, 1979.

THE DEPRESSION

Boardman, Fon Wyman. *The Thirties: America and the Great Depression*. New York: H.Z. Walck, 1967.

Goldston, Robert. *The Great Depression*. Indianapolis: Bobbs-Merrill, 1968.

Goslin, Ryllis Alexander and Omar Pancoast Goslin. *Rich Man, Poor Man: Pictures of a Paradox*. New York: Harper and Brothers, 1935.

Horan, James D. *The Desperate Years*. New York: Crown Publishers, 1962.

Katz, William Loren. *An Album of the Great Depression*. New York: Franklin Watts, 1970.

Other Works Consulted

Bettman, Otto L. *The Good Old Days, They Were Terrible*. New York: Random House, 1974.

Brunner, Karl. *The Great Depression Revisited*. Boston: Martinus Nijoff Publishing, 1981.

Congdon, Don. *The Thirties, A Time to Remember*. New York: Simon and Schuster, 1962.

Freidel, Frank. *The New Deal*. Englewood Cliffs, N.J.: Prentice-Hall, 1964.

Galbraith, John Kenneth. *The Great Crash*. Boston: Houghton Mifflin, 1972.

Miller, S.M. and Donald Tomaskovic-Devey. *Recapitalizing America, Alternatives to the Corporate Distortion of National Policy*. Boston: Routledge and Kegan, 1983.

Nash, Roderic. *The Nervous Generation: American Thought, 1917-1930*. Chicago: Rand McNally, 1970.

Saint-Etienne, Christian. *The Great Depression, 1929-1938: Lessons for the 1980s*. Stanford, Calif.: Hoover Institute Press, 1984.

Terkel, Studs. *Hard Times*. New York: Pantheon Books, 1970.

Index

Co-author Ronald Migneco is a screenwriter who lives in San Diego. Born and raised in St. Louis, Missouri, he acquired his college education at Grossmont College and San Diego State University. This is his first book.

Co-author Timothy Levi Biel was born and raised in eastern Montana. A graduate of Rocky Mountain College, he holds a Ph.D. in literary studies from Washington State University. He is the author of numerous nonfiction books, including *Pompeii: World Disasters* and *The Black Death: World Disasters*.

Illustrations designed by Maurie Manning capture the drama of the events described in this book.

Manning majored in illustration at Massachusetts College of Art in Boston and has been a professional children's illustrator for more than six years. Her work appears regularly in such magazines as *Children's Digest, Humpty Dumpty,* and *Highlights for Children.*

Manning was assisted by a team of three artists: Michael Spackman, Robert Caldwell, and Randol Eagles. A professional painter for more than nineteen years, Michael Spackman received his training at the High Museum Academy of Art in Atlanta. Robert Caldwell, a graduate of Syracuse University with a degree in fine arts, has been a fine arts professional for eight years. Randol Eagles is a specialist in figurative illustration, and has been a professional illustrator for three years.

Credits

Photo on page 20 courtesy of
New York Stock Exchange Archives,
New York, New York.

Photos on pages 37 and 43 courtesy of
Brown Brothers,
Sterling, Pennsylvania.

Photos on pages 49 and 55 by Arthur Rothstein,
The Depression Years, courtesy of
Dover Publications,
New York, New York.

Cartoon on page 26 courtesy of
Chicago Tribune,
Chicago, Illinois.

Cartoons on pages 35 and 48 courtesy of
The New Yorker,
New York, New York.